CARING FOR EMANUEL

By

Gloria Samuel

RB
Rossendale Books

Published by Lulu Enterprises Inc.
3101 Hillsborough Street
Suite 210
Raleigh, NC 27607-5436
United States of America

Published in paperback 2014

Copyright © Gloria Samuel 2014
ISBN: 978-1-291-88172-1

ABOUT THE AUTHOR

Gloria Samuel is a loving but persistent single-minded person. Her single-mindedness comes from the text in the bible that says 'a double-minded person is unstable in all their ways.' Her career stems from youth and community worker, pastoring, and missionary work. She has now taken to writing which she thoroughly enjoys.

DEDICATION

This book is dedicated to Emanuel the man at the center of the story, and to all those suffering from diabetes. It has been predicted that by 2030 there will be 552 million people, or 9.9% of adults with diabetes. The current known population of people with diabetes in the UK is 2.9 million. Foot problems account for the largest number of bed days used by diabetics in hospital. I also wish to thank my publisher Vincent Walsh for his guidance and words of wisdom whenever I needed encouragement.

FOREWORD

This story is based on my experience of caring for Mr. Emanuel Jones with type 2 diabetes mellitus, but will include other research material from library base material, internet and other sources. I will refer to him as Mr. A. Diabetes Mellitus is a condition in which the amount of glucose (sugar) in the blood is too high and the body cannot work as it normally should. Glucose comes from the digestion of starchy foods such as bread, rice, pasta, potatoes, chapattis, yams, plantain, sugars and other sweet foods. The pancreas in our body makes insulin.

Mr. E suffers from type 2 diabetes. He has had this disease for over 13 years. I met Mr. E in the 10th year of his disease in 2011. At the time of meeting him, he appeared a fit healthy middle-aged man but a little on the slim side. Through this chance meeting, or as some would say provident encounter, we became very good friends. After about three months of knowing Mr. E I discovered he was a diabetic.

Mr. E was taking a variety of medication. I had no former knowledge about this disease. My only thought was God had brought him in to me to take care of him and to convert him to Christianity. We became friends and eventually he told me he suffered from diabetes. Because no other person was taking responsibility for his health care I decided to take up the challenge and help him with his personal health care. It was through the practical running about doing basic mundane daily chores for him and questioning him about his state of health that I became interested in his diabetes.

Type 1 diabetes
Type 1 diabetes is called insulin dependent diabetes. This type of diabetes usually appears before the age of 40. It is treated by insulin injection, diet and exercise.

Type 2 diabetes
Type 2 diabetes is called non-insulin dependent diabetes. This is when the body can still make some insulin but not enough, or when the insulin that is produced does not work properly (known as insulin resistance). Diabetes is treated by insulin injection to normalize blood glucose. A

healthy life style and healthy eating can reduce the risk of damage to the kidneys, nerve damage, heart and artery problems.

Gloria Bevney
29TH JANUARY 2014

CHAPTER 1

During my caring for Mr. E and being in constant contact with him, I began my researching into the disease. Diabetes is a deficiency in the body, which means for those with type 2 diabetes the body is not able to convert enough glucose (sugar) into energy. Glucose is the main energy source for the body. When food is digested, it changes into energy, fats, protein and enzymes. The food we eat that affects blood sugar are carbohydrates. Carbohydrates when digested change into glucose. Food that contains carbohydrates include bread, rice, pasta, potatoes, yams, plantain, corn, fruits and dairy products.

Mr. E was showing me extra special attention and it became very clear that he fancied me. For me I curiously wanted to know more about his condition. But most of all, I was quite impressed about the amount of attention he was showing me. Even if it meant listening to his many past life stories of his earlier years in Jamaica.

People With Type 2 diabetes can eat carbohydrates but should use moderation when doing so. Carbohydrates produces glucose in our bodies, the glucose is then transferred to the blood and used for energy by our cells. In order for the glucose to transfer to the cells from our blood, the hormone insulin is needed. Insulin is produced by our beta cells in the pancreas. The pancreas is an organ in the body that produces insulin. This process is impaired when a person has diabetes.

Diabetes develops when the pancreas fails to produce insulin in the case of type 1 juvenile diabetes. Or it is producing insulin as in type 2 diabetes but the insulin it produces is not reaching the blood cells in the body to make it work sufficiently.

There are 2 types of diabetics.
Type 1 diabetes develops when the insulin is defective and cannot move glucose to the blood cells. Type 2 diabetes develops because either the insulin produced is not sufficient or is defective and cannot move the glucose into the cells. Type 2 diabetes is much more common and accounts for 90-95% of all diabetes. Type 2 diabetes is mainly found in adults over 50 but recently it has been

noted in children due to physical inactivity and obesity.

What are the symptoms of diabetes?
The symptoms of diabetes are: blurred vision, unusual thirst, frequent urination, slow healing cuts, unexplained tiredness, rapid weight loss, erectile dysfunction and numbness or tingling in hands or feet. All of these signs were prevalent or became noticeable during my caring for Mr. A. Mr. E then became my research subject for my MSc at University College London (UCL). Mr. E has type 2 diabetes. The above symptoms may occur rapidly in type 1 diabetes but with type 2 diabetes the onset is insidious (gradual and harmful) and is less noticeable.

CHAPTER 2

What are the treatments for diabetes? Some medical professionals say that there is no cure for either type of diabetes, and diabetic treatments and drugs are designed to help those with diabetes have a better quality of life, and to help the body control its glucose levels in the blood cells. There are two types of insulin. Insulin as part and human insulin. Insulin as part is insulin extracted from animals such as cows. And human insulin is formulated and developed in labs by scientists through genetic engineering of yeast. Recumbent Insulin.

Glucose level
Good control of glucose levels is the key to avoiding diabetic complications. Herbalist and meditative personnel say that there are herbal cures and remedies out there for diabetes. I'm of the belief and opinion that there are cures for every sickness on planet earth. This notion may appear as utopian in the mind of many. While there are those who believe that some diseases will never be cured because of individual past sins. No comment! This gives rise to the stories where it

has been said that some people have been cured of their disease because their sins are not as great as others. Whilst others would argue and say that some people will never be cured because they are too wicked and evil. This opinion comes mainly from religious communities.

I am yet to investigate how many people have been cured of their diabetes compared to how many have not. And what the statistical analysts have to say on the subject. When I met Mr. E in January 2011 he had not taken any serious steps to controlling his diabetes. And this eventually led to him developing diabetic foot ulcers and to the eventual amputation of his right foot below the knee, and of the two last toes on his left foot. My study needs further research into the working of amputation, the job of the Podiatrist/Chiropodist and the physiological effects on the patient, especially phantom limbs. I was relieved of my responsibility of taking care of Mr. E due to family differences and the amount of time Mr. E and I were spending together.

I have not seen Mr. E since April 2013
At the time of writing up this information I had not seen Mr. E since April 2013 his ex-wife who abandoned him during his illness suddenly showed

up and became increasingly upset about the care and attention I was showing to Mr. A, and vice versa, and called the police on myself and instructed Mr. E to stop seeing me. Mr. E then told me during one of my hospital visits to him in his time of crisis, that I would have to be 'The patsy' and take the blame for the present problems stirred up by his ex-wife in order to maintain the peace. So for the sake of peace and the intervention of the local police who instructed me to stop seeing Mr. A. I gave up visiting him and decided to write about my experience with him from memory.

CHAPTER 3

People with diabetes require insulin injection to replace the insulin missing from the body. It calls for a balancing of food and insulin intake alongside physical activities. Diabetics need to work with a team of medical experts in the field of diabetic care. These experts are there to assist with the medical, educational and management of diabetics. I met many of Mr. E's medical treatment team. They included a number of people:

Diabetes team : Should normally include spouses, doctors, nurses, dietician, physiotherapist, carers, parents, friends, relatives and anyone who supports the diabetic care plan.

Fundoscope: When the pupils of the eyes are dilated with drops and a health care professional will check them for vessel change.

Hypoglycaemia: (hypo) low blood glucose (sugar) level; below 4 mmol/l.

Ketones: Dangerous chemicals which can be produced in the blood if the blood glucose (sugar) level is too high.

Opthamologist: Doctor with specialist training in the diagnosis and treatment of diabetic complications, especially those that affect the eyes.

Optometrist: Person trained to perform eye examination and test for eye problems. They do not treat eye disorder. That is the job of the ophthalmologist.

Podiatrist/Chiropodist: Person with expert knowledge in foot care/lower limb. I was discharged of my duties of caring for Mr. E after the amputation of his lower right foot and his two last toes on his left feet. I did not experience meeting with the Podiatrist/Chiropodist nor do I have any information about this side of his treatment.

This area of investigation needs further study.

Treatment
Type 2 diabetes treatment varies depending on the blood glucose level. Most patients are counseled

to change their life style and lose weight. It is important to work with your doctor, diabetic nurse or professional dietician and other medical professionals.

Treatment begins with changing certain food choices and the beginning of a diabetic programme. Diabetes is a progressive disease and treatment may change over time, some may require oral medication, or insulin injection. It is best to speak with your doctor or medical diabetic team over a length of time until the disease is under control, and a medicinal programmer is in place. This should be monitored or assessed every six months.

CHAPTER 4

When I met Mr. E he was already on insulin both orally and by subcutaneous injection, injecting himself with insulin below the skin but not into the muscles. Mr. E had lost quite a lot of weight compared with previous photographs I had seen of him.

I decided to take up the challenge to provide and assist him with the nursing care he needed that was necessary for both his mental and physical health. Especially since we had become friends. All human behavior is aimed towards the satisfaction of our basic human needs be it.

- Physical needs
- Emotional needs
- Massage
- Social needs

Our physical needs are closely related to our bodily functions and are sometimes primary or physiologically driven. Our physical needs include food, water, oxygen, stimulation, clothing and shelter for our bodily warmth and protection. Our activities or sensory motor stimulation includes sex, physical exercise and rest. Whilst caring for Mr. E his diabetes became worse and I also became his cook, cleaner and did most of his everyday chores, such as his shopping for groceries, toiletries and his clothing.

Early in the mornings I would go downstairs to Mr. E's apartment to visit him and to check on his health. I noticed he had turned the mop bucket into a urinal. He was often too weak or too tired to get out of bed to go to the toilet. It was normal for me to find a half-full bucket of pee in his room each morning. Not knowing a lot about diabetes and not knowing excessive urine was a typical sign of diabetes, I naturally assumed that he was very lazy and believed that he saw me as someone to freeload from to aid his recovery, or someone to do all his administrative running about. Not knowing that Mr. E's bladder was constantly being refilled and he was up half the night expelling urine from his body. Mr. E would never explain to me about his diabetes. Everything I learned and observed about his sickness was through trial and error. He'd excluded me from many aspects of his private life of diabetes and all that comes with the territory.

When Mr. E moved into the apartment a year after I was there, most of us living on the premises were either students, low-wagers, unemployed or homeless. He was given a room directly beneath mine. Mr. E would play reggae music all the time. His music choice was mostly from the 60's - 90's. He reminded me of those old has-been codgers who had lived their lives and were reminiscing on 'The Good Old Days' be it good or bad times. I am sure I reminded him of those deserted lonely middle-age married women who just needed 'A good seeing to.' as he would often hint out loudly to me.

CHAPTER 5

Some days I would get so mad at him for having his music turned up so loud as it continually ascended through my roof and echoed through the walls and ceiling. I would retaliate by turning my music up to counteract his sounds. Then one day I went down to his apartment, knocked on his door, and confronted him about how loud his music was and at the same time handed him a hand full of music that I enjoyed listening to.

This was a challenging moment for me because although Mr. E suffered from type 2 diabetes he was 'No easy push-over', quite the reverse. As a matter of fact I was very much afraid of him and was terrified to confront him about his loud music. And knowing myself I wasn't going to go to management to complain about him or any other tenant in the building. So I just took courage and went down to speak to him myself about his loud music. To me he was causing noise pollution and I wasn't having it.

Most persons living in close proximity to Mr. E were music lovers, and they played music all the time. That was one good thing I remembered about that accommodation. It was after confronting him about his loud music that we really became friends. He admired my brazen feistiness in standing up to him. By visiting him often, I eventually learned that people with diabetes have excessive thirst, urinate a lot, dry skin, have blurred vision, tingling sensation in their feet and felt weak because of low blood glucose. His kidney was busy at night eliminating built-up ketones, cholesterol and excessive residue from his body by the process of urination elimination.

Mr. E's diabetes made him excessively thirsty, dehydrated and sometimes stressful. His relief from the stress of the diabetes was to play and listen to music all the time. I assumed Mr. E had given up on life and just couldn't be bothered any more. Whereas in fact Mr. E had become dehydrated during the night and was too weak to get up out of bed on most mornings. Diabetes can give many sleepless nights if not controlled. He battled most nights with urination. Mr. E was always thirsty and water becomes more than just a normal physical need.

Emotional needs

Our emotional needs are closely interwoven with our physical needs and these needs are met by our interaction with others. This includes love, approval, and esteem. Whilst caring for Mr. E I noticed he was a very interesting person.

Like the great man Jesus, Mr. E had a variety of interesting stories to tell. He was also a great listener. He spoke of his past life with passion and conviction. His conquest of women, his social and political life in Jamaica were real adventure stories for me to listen to. His jobs, his restaurant business, his travels and his family life were all very interesting tales. Diabetes does not discriminate it is not confined to one particular race. It has now become a global problem. Today's figures show that 1 person in every 1,000 has the disease. I blame it on the amount of genetically modified food crops that we consume by the tons that are engineered just for profit. It's all about profit and less about the individual's personal needs.

CHAPTER 6

I could not provide Mr. E's sexual need. My faith in God and my religion prevented me from having sex with him. Although many people have faith, believe in God and have sex, I was too afraid to venture down that road with Mr. A. Mr. E had propositioned me about sex on numerous occasions. I was afraid because I knew in my mind I had an estranged husband out there somewhere in the world. My own emotional needs were being met by listening to Mr. E's stories; and I was meeting some of his emotional needs by providing him with daily health care and attention with the occasional foot and back massage.

Massage
Massage treatment is good for diabetics. It involved rubbing and kneading his muscles. It gave him relief and comfort from the tingling sensation he was experiencing in his hands, feet and legs. I would normally perform this treatment as our daily meal was being cooked in the oven to work up an appetite. The massage I gave Mr. E was therapeutic and it relieved him of some of his muscular and nerve pain.

My emotional need was also being met by having someone around to talk to. Love and emotions is something that cannot be forced on an individual. I loved Mr. E but I was not in love with him. I enjoyed being around him. But I couldn't be inside him. On most days I was worn-out just taking personal care of him, pushing him about in his wheel chair that we had eventually borrowed from a hospital foyer. Going from one hospital appointment to the next. Our emotional needs include recognition, loyalty, respect and trust. This can also apply to the patient's perception of his health carers, be it doctors, nursing staff or family members.

Whilst Mr. E was in hospital I observed nursing staff with different outlooks and different methods of applying their nursing practice. Likewise those with different ways of interacting with patients. All nurses were acting in a trained professional manner but the social-economic background of many nurses played a very great part in their perceived attitude toward patients care.

There were nurses who were ambitious and career driven. All they really cared about was their career. These were what I term as 'figure number crunching nurses' they ticked all the right boxes and had no other goal than to meet administrative targets. There were nurses who were quite contented in their position doing their best to make the recovery life of their hospitalised patient less frightening and more at ease. I observed there were nurses who worked with an air of superiority towards lower social-economic black patients. These were mainly nurses from Western European countries. They looked down on black and Asian patients, but they were often too frightened and intimidated by the white English patients.

CHAPTER 7

There were nurses with the attitude of 'I'm only here to do my required number of hours and when that's over 'I am out of here, because I have a life outside the NHS.' These were mainly younger trainee auxiliary nursing staff. The importance of being employed and having a job in a time of recession was not a priority in their thinking process.

There was a nurse who had been in the NHS system for so long, and the job had become so mundane that she had not noticed that the hospital system she was working in had changed. She was clearly living in the past 'the good old days of nursing practices'. Today working for the NHS is no longer a 'job for life.' I spoke to one head of nursing staff who had not realised that the hospital she had worked in for over 20 years had now become a teaching hospital. She was clearly in her own world. When patients are sick the nursing care they receive makes a huge difference to their recovery. If a patient feels that the nursing or care professional do not respect him/her, they may become very demanding, he/she may become withdrawn and not co-operate with efforts to make them well again.

The emotional needs of a patient includes self-sufficiency and the need to be needed and wanted. Most nursing professionals have the attitude of I am the professional and you the patient don't really know much about your own body. But I have come to realise that most patients are aware of the workings of their own bodies and see hospitals as a repair shop to visit when their body is not functioning correctly. But on entering this repair shop, the patient is expecting to be treated with respect. When a carer or a nursing professional do not know or has no specialised training in a particular field of nursing, more often than not the patient becomes a statistical figure and is treated like one.

Whilst Mr. E was in hospital for his diabetes, at times he felt like he was in a four star hotel getting the best medical treatment and at other times he felt like he was a prisoner being vilified by the nurses. In the span of one year I had escorted Mr. E to four hospitals, and attended other health appointments and wrote letters on his behalf.

I was watching a medical drama crime scene. There was a clip where by the detective was investigating a missing person. He got a forensic artist to construct a sculptural model of what the missing person would look like seventeen years later. After publicizing the photograph in the media, he was able to locate the place where the runaway youth had once lodged. The manager of the homeless youth project was asked by the detective if he could remember or identify the missing person by the photograph or put a name to the face of the individual. The manager of the youth project replied by saying 'in the past he would try to get to know every person that came into the center by name'. The crime scene detective then interjected and finished his sentence by saying 'after a while all the faces that comes to the center start to look alike.' I took note and concluded that this was the general outlook for most long-term employers who come in daily contact with the public. Be it doctors, nurses, teachers, youth leaders, bankers, business men, shop keepers etc. After a while all individuals of certain races start to look the same. But this should not take away the need to show respect and be respectful to others in your care. Our emotional need to be productive and creative is always with us. The majority of patients want to get better in order to continue contributing to life including those with diabetes although this contribution may now be impaired. Mr. E after being personally cared for, supported and respected by myself for two years, eventually told me he was now ready to seriously learn about his illness to improve his health.

He had been diagnosed with type 2 diabetes for over 10 years when I came to know him in January 2011. He was not taking care of his diabetes. He had allowed himself to get to the stage where a diabetic foot ulcer had developed and needed to be amputated. He was eventually amputated below the right knees, and had the removal of the last two toes on the left foot in 2012. I met Mr. E when he appeared quite fit and healthy but below the surface appearance he was obviously quite ill and was masking good health. He was taking his diabetes medication erratically that resulted in the above medical operation.

Social needs

We all have social needs. Mr. E's social needs remained constant after his operation but with some mechanical and emotional adjustments due to the diabetes. For example he loved music but sometimes was unable to get up and put the music on because he was bed-ridden. The music had to be placed near his bedside with headphones where it was easily accessible. During the stage of Mr. E's being bed-ridden in hospital he also had to be bed-bathed and fed in bed and this bought about the realization of the loss of some of his independence.

There are many thoughts that go on in a person's mind when they lose their mobility. The first thought is to get well. Followed by negative thoughts of becoming immobile, dependent, and degenerate. The latter being the most dominant thought in the mind of the patient who becomes immobile. In such cases the health care professionals, psychologist, and non-professionals all have to play a part in strengthening the patient's mind by being positive in their outlook towards the patient and project healthy thoughts and feeling to the patient.

CHAPTER 8

At this stage of emotional turmoil the nursing professionals can either become saints or a hindrance in the eyes of the patient. There were times when I felt that Mr. E was thinking, all I was fit for was to clean up after him. When I had these thoughts and feelings I would call on his carers or nursing staff to take care of him because they were being paid to do so, whilst I was not. I would then play a more socially active role such as selecting his music or going out and purchasing take-away foods as he could not get out of bed.

Mr. E's social needs were not hard to identify. I assisted in getting him up in the mornings when he was at home, washed, dressed, and made his breakfast, preparing his lunch, and evening meals, made sure he had his music, topping up his mobile phone and went about from hospital to hospital for appointments. Most days we purchased take-away meals. On occasions I would cook him a meal and take it to him while he was in the hospital.

One particular hospital served a good variety of daily meals so I did not have to travel far to purchase a meal for him. Like I've mentioned before there was no sex between us, but I'd hugged and kissed his face and forehead on numerous occasions making sure that I never kissed his lips. These moments helped with our social emotional needs. Nature teaches us that social contact plays a big role in our mental stimulation and development. Most people in the Western world today pay more attention to their gadgets, such as their computers and mobile phones games than they do with human contact. The time spent on electronic gadgets out strips human contact, touch and interaction.

Mr. E had become so accustomed to me that psychologically he only wanted to wear the clothing I had bought for him. He cherished those items like a child with a favorite toy. My physical caring and natural mind healing through the power of God had influenced Mr. E so much that he only wanted to wear the clothing that I had purchased and touched. He felt they had some great spiritual healing calming effect to them. I projected these feelings and thoughts to him. Mr. E was meeting my social needs. I felt alive in his company listening to his stories about his past life or about the events of his day prior to seeing him. Social stimulation produces chemicals in the brain that aid towards our wellbeing. Every day I looked forward to seeing Mr. E whilst he was in hospital. But his amputation due to the diabetes threw me off balance; it was one of the worst crises in my life. I had never been that close to anyone who was sick before and it led me to a dark place in my mind. I couldn't understand why God had not healed him, even though I had offered up many prayers for him. I would spend nights crying on my bed, I became a total wreck. I was so upset I blamed the doctors and nurses who agreed to perform the operation on Mr. E's foot contrary to my advice on alternative healing that I'd informed him and them about. The doctors and nurses in that particular hospital and on that ward then became 'the enemy.' Paranoia had entered the good place in my mind that was preserved for natural and spiritual healing. But as they say in some circles, 'paranoia IS the finer point of the truth.'

CHAPTER 9

I was an emotional wreck and I couldn't see the wood for the trees. But after about nine or so months of emotional turmoil and separation from Mr. E because of a family disputes over my care for him, I began to pick myself up and decided to use the situation to write about his hospital care, his medical care, his diabetes and his medication. Mr. E's social needs were identified as caring for him, his music and belonging. Socially he had originally come from the Tottenham area. He began distancing himself from that group of people as he was conscious of his diabetes amputation and the possibility of being mocked at by some of his peers who knew and respected him whilst he was healthy. These feelings were reinforced, made plain and obvious when a family members phoned and told him about other people in the area whose status in life had degenerated due to ill health. 'Humans can be so cruel.'

I on the other hand I did not see things in this light. I equated his sickness as a man who was suffering for righteousness sake and for his family. And this became my conscious thoughts throughout his suffering. Mr. E had become a bit like Eyesus/Jesus in my mind. Was I in love with Mr. A? I would say that Mr. E was a man of suffering. And he was suffering to keep others safe. My religious belief has great influence in my thinking. Providence had brought Mr. E in my path to care for him. And no sooner had I become accustomed to looking after him, 'they' snatch him from me. How cruel was that!

There is a story of a man who had bought his daughter two dogs for her birthday, they were puppies and he allowed her to play with them and treated them with all good things. Then one day when the father noticed that the daughter had become fond of the puppies and was playing happily with them. He decided to kill one of the dogs by wringing its neck in front of the little girl. It was a very cruel thing to do. From that day forward his daughter was unable to love any other pet given to her by her father for fear that it would one day be killed or taken from her leaving her heartbroken. So yes! I'd loved him with a question mark. Because I had no clue 'where my estranged husband was'. But when the relationship with Mr. E was killed by the cruel act of his relatives I had learned my lesson not to allow another person under my skin. A theory that has yet to be proven when I next see my estranged husband.

Mr. E my diabetic friend once told me that he and I would never separate and we would always be together one way of another. I took that to mean that if he wasn't with me physically he would always be there for me spiritually. But as they say in the world of medical and forensic science it's the physical evidence that counts regardless of our intuition. After being separated from Mr. E and his diabetes, I suddenly found myself being attracted to men in wheel chairs. During the process of my research investigation on the subject of diabetes mellitus, I met a young man, let's call him Mr. K.

CHAPTER 10

He was coming from the library as I was going to it. He was in his wheelchair by the traffic lights waiting for the lights to change and we both stood there in silence. I plucked up courage and asked him what was wrong with him. He said he suffered from Multiple Sclerosis (MS) and we chatted until the lights changed. He said he'd just taken a book from the library about his illness and wanted to read up about it. When we parted company I said to myself 'My how strange, he looks so much like Mr. E with the diabetes who was ripped away from me by his people.'

At this point my pains of missing Mr. E with the diabetes were coming to an end. Mr. K was living quite close to me and he then become another subject of fascination. From there on I kept bumping into Mr. K with the Multiple Sclerosis (MS) on the high street and we chatted to each other. He invited me to his home and we became friends, then we fell out because he wanted to sleep with me and I would not allow him to. He then stopped speaking altogether. So I figured 'What the hell,' the best thing for me to do at this time was just to continue writing up learned experiences about Mr. E's diabetic care, his medication and recovery.

I spent approximately two years and three months caring for Mr. E with type 2 diabetes and in that space of time he spent roughly one year and three months in hospital. We went from one hospital to the next, in all I had experience visiting four hospitals with him and one health clinic on his behalf. All in relation to his diabetes or hypoglycaemia when his blood glucose became too low or he had passed out.

We attended Moorefield's eye hospital for his diabetic neuropathy, a disease of the nerves in his eyes, a degeneration of the eye nerves. This was diagnosed in New Ham University Hospital where laser treatment had started but he was later sent to Moorefield's eye hospital for more tests and finally to Whipps Cross Hospital, and was placed under a eye consultant for a minor operation. I was with Mr. E at the hospitals on most days until evening when visiting time was over. The nurses and doctors saw my keenness and interest in Mr. E's care and recovery, they allowed me to spend all day with him until evening visiting time was over.

They were also afraid of him especially when he would 'Act Up on not seeing me.'

I washed him, bathed and fed him when he couldn't care for himself especially during the time of his tuberculosis (TB) when he was isolated from other patients and couldn't be in contact with patients and visitors in the general ward. The patient ward unit was where Mr. E received his medical and nursing care. It became the place where he lived for little over a year. This area I observed was maintained as a safe, pleasant, clean and orderly environment for his physical and mental wellbeing. As should be the case at most hospitals. Constant effort is needed to achieve and maintain the necessary order and sanitation in hospitals. The Patient Care Unit whilst Mr. E was in hospital is standard in most hospitals in London UK.

CHAPTER 11

I observed that the hospital equipment consisted of:
   Bed
   Overhead light
   Over bed-table
   Chairs

The following linens provided
   Bed linen
   Towels
   Wash Cloth
   Blankets

Toilet equipment included:
   Wash Basin
   Soap
   Emesis basin (to vomit in)
   Bed-pans
   Urinal
   Toilet paper

Other articles were:
   Water pitcher
   Unbreakable glass
   Bedside call button

Most days I assisted in providing Mr. E with basic hygiene care which was undoubtedly one of the most important nursing activities. Patient hygiene contributes immeasurably to a patient's feeling of emotional well-being and Mr. E was no different.

APPENDIX 1

Symptoms of diabetes :

- Thirst
- Frequent Urination
- Tiredness or Lack of Energy
- Blurred Vision
- Thrush infection
- Weight Loss in Type 1 diabetes
- Erectile dysfunction

Normal Blood Glucose: (sugar is 3.5 - 7.8 mmol/l).

Diabetes Blood Glucose: 15mmol/l or higher.

Type 1 diabetes happens when the body's immune system destroys the cells in the pancreas.

Type 2 diabetes happens when the pancreas produces insulin but the insulin produced is not enough to reach all the cells in the body.

The Pancreas: Digestive or endocrine gland. A large elongated glandular organ lying near the stomach. It secretes juices into the small intestines and the hormone insulin, glucagons and somatostatin into the blood stream.

Insulin: the hormone that regulates glucose (sugar) level in the blood. From the Latin; Insula meaning Island: After the "Islet of Langerhans".

Antibodies: Are proteins that fights infections. A protein that is produces by B cells in the body in response to the presence of antigen i.e. a bacterium or virus.
Antibodies are a prime of immune response in resistance to disease and acts by attaching foreign antigen and weakening and destroying it.

It is thought that a virus or chemical may be responsible for triggering this response in people with a genetic predisposition.

Genetic: Involving or resulting from genes.

Cells: biology; basic unit of living things, the smallest individual functioning unit in the structure of an organism usually consisting of one or more nuclei surrounded by cytoplasm and enclosed by membranes. Cells also contains organelles, such as mitochondria, lysosomes and ribosome.

Nitrate: Chemical groups of salt or ester of nitric acid.

Organelles: A special part of a cell that has its own function; e.g. the special part of the mitochondria.

Mitochondria: A small or rod shape body that is found in the cytoplasm of most cells or products enzymes for the metabolic conversion from food to energy.

Proteins: A complex natural compound that has globular or fibrous composed of linked amino acids. Proteins are essential to all living cells and virus. food sources that is rich in protein are molecules. A balance diet of fresh fruits, vegetables, meat and fish help to warn of infection. Meat and fish is full of protein.

Meat:
1. Edible animal flesh, especially that of mammal or birds.
2. Edible fruit or nut parts inside a shell or rind.

Rind:
Tough outside layer of a fruit.

Fish:
1. Water vertebrates with guilds and has jaws, fin, scales, and a slender body. It has a two chambered heart, and gills for providing oxygen to the blood.
2. Consumed for food. Either cooked or raw.

APPENDIX 2   Mr E's Medication

Here is a list of medications Mr E was taking whist hospitalised:

> Gabapentin
> Novorapid flex pen injection
> Bisoprolol Fumarate
> Simvastatin
> Paracetamol
> Carbomer Gel (eye drops)
> Amlodipine
> Vitamin B Compound
> Enoxaparin Sodium Syringe
> Aspirin
> Lantus Solo Star
> 100 units /m/ solution injection
> Laxido

Gabapentin

Also called neurotine is a medicine that has been approved by the Food and Drug Administration to treat partial and secondary seizure in adults and children 12 years of age and older. And to treat children with partial seizures age 3-12. It is normally administered with other seizer medications. During my personal care for Mr. A, he had 1 seizers and other feverish tremors. The ambulance and paramedics was called for him to be admitted to hospital. Gabapentin has been approved to treat pains of postherpetic neuralgic. 'Nerve pain.' I was naive about Mr. E's diabetes and was not fully conscious about the true nature of his illness and naturally I assumed he was 'faking it' to get my attention.

It was not until I decided to take it upon myself to research his condition of type 2 diabetes that I began to have some understanding of what he was going through.

Even though I had access to Mr. E's medical notes on several occasions, I did not read up on them because I was pre-occupied with getting him better. Getting Mr. E physical fit again was my main motivation in helping him. Plus it never occurred to me to read up his hospital notes even though at times I alone escorted him to the other hospital appointments in the ambulance without a nursing staff present, and his notes were handed over to me by the nurse to be handed over to admission at the other hospital appointments. Especially when they were short-staffed. But with Mr. E's permission I note down all his medication that was on his bedside table whiles in hospital just for the sake of simply knowing what he was taking and what I had to be aware of administering to him when the time came for him to be discharged from hospital.

Mr. E was prescribed new medicines by his doctors during his hospital stay. The doctors prescribed a fresh batch of medication and placed the old batch of medicines he took to the hospital with him in locker for when he was to be discharged. Gabapentin being the first on my list of Mr. E's medications. This medicine is said to be excreted by the kidney and the doses or the way it is administered may differ from patient to patient. (Original brand name Neurontin). For people with nervous disorder. What they mean by being excreted by the kidney is another line of study in itself as I have no idea what this really means. Gabapentin is an hormone that's excreted from the kidney and recumbent? Gabapentin is also available in generic form. Which means that it is made in labatories by scientist in pharmaceutical companies by means of genetic modification?

49

Gabapentin can look different in colour, depending on the company who makes it. Some are clear and water like whilst others are cloudy looking.

Mr. E Was Taking Nova Rapid Flex Pen Injection

Nova Rapid Flex Pen is insulin aspart. Insulin as part is insulin that is extracted from animals such as the cow, where as human insulin is genetically made. Novo Rapid is used to treat diabetes mellitus in adults and children. Diabetes mellitus is a condition where your pancreas does not produce enough insulin to control your blood glucose (sugar) level. Therefore extra insulin is needed. There are two types of diabetes mellitus. Type 1 diabetes is called juvenile on-set diabetes.

Type 2 diabetes is called mature diabetes.

Patient with type 1 diabetes always requires insulin to control their blood glucose level. Some patient with type 2 diabetes may also require insulin treatment with diet, exercise and tablets. Mr. E has been taking Novo Rapid Flex Pen insulin for a number of years and was doing some exercise whilst taking the drug, but at times he would cut down on his exercise due to nerve pain. Novo Rapid lowers blood glucose. After injection the onset of Novo Rapid has a maximum effect of 1-3 hours, and the effect may last for up to 5 hours.

As with all insulin the duration of action will vary according to the doses, injection site, blood flow, temperature, and level of physical activity. Mr. E was not engaged in any rigorous exercise when I met him. He did some exercise whilst lying on his bed such as sit-ups, knee bending, and muscle flexing. Due to the short duration of action Novo Rapid has a lower risk of causing nocturnal hypoglycemic episode. 'Night Black-Outs.' Novo Rapid Flex Pen is a pre-filled dial-a dose insulin pen. It is able to deliver from 1-60 units in increments of 1 unit of insulin. Novo Rapid is said to be non-addictive. But like most food and drugs, a level of addiction is possible. Mr. E was prescribed Novo Rapid by his doctor for his diabetes. This insulin is only available by prescription. Patients should be encouraged to discussed and ask question about their medication with their doctor, diabetic nurse or pharmacist. Mr. E knew his medications and doses but was not taking them as prescribed. Especially if he had fasted and had gone without breakfast or had overslept because of being up all night with urinary problems.

Novo Rapid should not be used if you have an allergic reaction which may include redness, swelling, rash, itching at the injection site, shortness of breath, wheezing or difficulty in breathing, swelling of the face, lips, tongue or other parts of the body. If a patients has a lot of hypo episodes you will need to discuss the appropriate form of treatment with your doctor. If you are not sure if you should be using this medication you should discuss it with your doctor. Many people are tempted to experiment with drugs and medicine that belongs to friends. Novo Rapid should not be used after the expired date on the package.

Before you start using Novo Rapid you should inform your doctor of any allergies to other medications, food preservatives or dyes. Whiles Mr. E was in hospital for his diabetes, it was discover that he had contracted tuberculosis (TB). He told me he must have caught the virus from friends some months back. I notice that Mr.

E's insulin injection regime had changed whilst being treated for TB. He was isolated from other patients in a single unit. Nurses, doctors and visitors wore protective mask and aprons whiles treating Mr. E's TB. I on the other hand like Mr. E did not wear the protected mask most of the time, unless a nurse firmly instructed me to do so.

I exercised my faith to show Mr. E that I was not afraid of the disease and Eyes us/Jesus was protecting me form all virus, germs and disease. May be I was being naïve, maybe I was acting in faith. But I had to prove to Mr. E that God is still in the healing and protection business. The episode of Mr. E's tuberculosis (TB) was an experience; he was prescribed and administered a barrage of drug treatments. Weather he was being given his insulin medicine intravenously needs further investigation. The nurses and doctors were constantly in and out of his room with various drugs, drips and cannulates, and it wasn't the usual finger-tip-pricking nor stomach injection that I normally observe. Mr. E was now on drips and blood transfusion, and he spent about a month in isolation.

When Mr. E's tuberculosis (TB) had being given the all cleared by the doctors, and he was transferred back onto the open ward. I was sent to NHS clinics to be tested to see if I had contracted his (TB) virus. I too was giving the all clear. I had not caught his virus of (TB). Back on the open ward he continued receiving cannulating drips into his veins and other treatments. Cannulations were administered with drugs into his veins. Mr. E was on canulating drugs treatment for months. He hated the dam thing and at times became very angry with the nurses and junior doctor for not finding his correct veins and getting the needle into it.

During his treatment Mr. E was placed on beta blocking agents, as used for the treatment of heart condition or high blood pressure. He was also on salicylate drugs e.g. aspirin, for the relief of nerve pain, lowering of fever, and reduction of blood clotting. When I first met Mr. E he was in his 10th year of diabetes treatment. His normal diabetic treatment continued after the tuberculosis (TB) had cleared up him.

BISOPROLOL
Mr. E's medication included Bisoprolol because he obviously had some slight heart problem. This medicine works by effecting the body response to some nerve impulses especially in the heart. I was with Mr. E when he underwent testing's for nerves impulse damage. The specialist doctor taped wires on his upper and lower arms and on his chest and took read-outs from a machine to measure his nerve reaction. The active ingredient in Bisoprolol is Bisoprolol Fumarate. [Bisoprolol Orion] belongs to a group of medicines call Beta-Blockers. As a result Bisoprolol slows the heart rate and makes the heart more effective at pumping blood around the body. Heart failure occurs when the heart muscles is weak and unable to pump enough blood supply that is needed for the body.

SIMVASTATIN
Mr. E was taking simvastatin medicine to lower his cholesterol. There are 'good' and 'bad' cholesterol. (LDL Cholesterol) is bad cholesterol which is a substance in the

blood called triglycerides. Simvastatin Tablets raises the level of 'good cholesterol' (HDL Cholesterol) for you to stay healthy. Although Mr. E had lost a considerable amount of weight for his height. There were times whiles in hospital when he had gained weight and had to be placed on Simvastatin to reduce his cholesterol.

THE SYMPTOMS OF DIABETES ARE:

Increase Thirst
Frequent Urination
Blurred Vision
Infection such as (Thrush)
Weight Loss

The symptoms of diabetes may not appear until blood glucose level are above 15mmol/l or higher. It is quite common to have diabetes without knowing it. In Australia one adult in twelve has diabetes. Research shows that for every person prescribed with diabetes there is another who has the disease but has not yet been diagnosed.

ENOXAPRIN
One of Mr. E's prescribed medications was Enoxaparin. Enoxaparin is also called Clexane. This medicine is administered by subcutaneous injection (under the skin but above the muscle). It is given to patient to prevent Deep Vein Thrombosis disease, or for the treatment of unstable angina, non-Q wave, myocardial infraction, and acute ST elevation through the arterial line of a dialysis circuit.

Enoxaparin is mainly given for the prevention of thrombus formation in the extra-corporeal circulation during haemodialysis and via intervention (bolus); injection through an intervention line. It is used only for initial dose of acute STEM indication and before PIC when needed. Enoxaparin must not be administered by intra-muscular rout. As Mr. E was on Enoxaparin which is normally administered via subcutaneous injection, (above the muscle but below the skin) and for the treatment of thrombus. I can only assume Mr. E was given this medication to prevent vein clotting. To avoid accidents the pre-filled syringe of Enoxaparin comes with an auto safety device.

Needle stick injury accident happens in hospitals or at home when needles are left opened and not discarded safely. Whiles tending to Mr. E's medical care in hospital, I was clearing up his bedside area and was suddenly pricked with an open-ended, a needle that a nurse had left on his bedside table. As instructed by the senior nurses I was told to go to Accident And Emergency (A&E) for a full blood test to see if I had been infect with any of Mr. E's germs or viruses. Once again I was given the all clear, but the situation was taken quite seriously, discussed and noted down by the nursing team on his ward.

LUMECARE - Car Bomer Gel.

Mr. E was prescribed Lumecare Car Bomer Gel for his diabetes retinopathy eye problem. He had been given laser eye treatment where doctors use a device admitting forced beams of light that utilizes the ability of substance to absorb electromagnetic energy and re-radiate it as a highly forced bean of synchronized wave length radiation to the eye. I had accompanied Mr. E to a number of these eye hospital appointments. At times he could see clearly and at other times he said he was only seeing shadows. I strongly advised Mr. E against laser eye surgery but as soon as my back was turned, he would do whatever he felts like and I just tag along with him.

Lumecare Carbomer Gel eye drops were administered to Mr. E as a part of his drug therapy for his eye condition. Lumecare - Carbomer Gel is a sterile transparent liquid eye gel containing 0.2% w/v carbomer disodum electrolytes, sorbitol, sodium, hydroxide, and the preservative cetrimide present in10g polyfoil tube. Carbomer Gel provides a smooth luxurious feeling for sore eyes with lasting soothing relief from grittiness, itching, burning, and foreign body sensation.

Lumecare Carbomer Gel

Can be used for dry eye sensation that is as a result of ocular surface disorder that can be caused by a number of different reasons, for example where the normal tears are either of poor quality or produced in too little quantity to keep the eye significantly moist. Symptom of dry eye sensation may also be produced by watching too much television and computer screens, infrequent blinking, and certain medical treatments including refractive laser surgery like those given to Mr. E during his hospitalisation, atmospheric pollution such as dry atmosphere air condition, central heating, wind and sun. All are conditions that can cause dry eye sensation. Lumecare Carbomer Gel is used when eyes become red and sore and begins to itch, feels gritty or burn that is caused by dry eyes. Place one drop of the gel into each eye 3-4 times a day or as directed by your doctor, pharmacist or optician.

To use Lumecare Carbomer Gel you should first wash your hands. If you wear contact lenses remove them and do not replace them until 30 minutes after the solution. Squeeze the tube gently until a small drop is formed, tilt your head back look up, pull down your eye lid and squeeze one drop of Lumecare Carbomer Gel into the gap between your eye and your eye lid. Blink a few times to spread the gel evenly over the surface and carefully wipe away any excess around the eye lid with a clean tissue.

POSSIBLE SIDE EFFECTS
Burning sensation in the eye which quickly passes. Blur vision immediately after use. Do not operate machinery, use electric tools, or drive a car until vision is restored.

STORAGE
Store out of reach of children. Do not store above 25oC. Does not use after the expiry date?

VITIMIN B COMPOUND
Mr. E was also on vitamin B compound. Weather these vitamins were strong or weak are something that needs further investigation. Vitamin B compound is used for tiredness a classic symptom of diabetes. Vitamin B compound is also used for the loss of function and the growth of new blood cells in the eyes to help restore vision. As Mr. E had gone through laser surgery so it was necessary for the recovery of his vision. Vitamin B compound is also used in the treatment of beri beri, a conditions caused by vitamin B thiamine deficiency.

Vitamin B compound plays a vital role in carbohydrate metabolism, it aids in the digestion of grains meat and yeast. Vitamin B compound is good for pellagra a disease caused by a dietary deficiency and a condition caused by nicotinamide deficiency. Before taking Vitamin B compound you should tell your doctors especially if you are allergic to or hypersensitive to nicotinamide, pyridoxine, hydrochloride, riboflavin, thiamine, or any other agent in vitamin B compound.

PARACETAMOL

Mr. E was also on paracetamol I suspect for his nerve pain. Paracetamol tablets belong to a group of medicines call analgesics. Paracetamol is used for the relief of mild to moderate pain and fever control. On three occasions I observed Mr. E suffering feverish tremors. The first time was when he blacked out over his toilet, the ambulance was called and they admitted him to hospital. The second time was while he was in hospital itself and was placed on the ward for stroke patients to be tested for any sign of stroke. The third time was when he was discharged from hospital and he had to be re-admitted. I called the ambulance they came and gave him on site attention before taking him to hospital.

Paracetamol is also used for toothaches, colds, influenza, joint pains and period pains. You should inform your doctor if you are taking paracetamol especially if you are allergic to the ingredients in the tablet and if you have suffered from alcoholism. Mr. E did not tell me that he had once suffered from alcoholism. It was his doctor who presumed that I knew of his pass condition that informed me of it. I kept his alcoholism secret to myself for the sake of not wanted to disclose the information to Mr. E in order not to make him feel guilty or embarrass and in any case I am not his judge. You should inform your doctor if you are taking other medications with paracetamol. More often than not Mr. E did not go into any detail with me about the medicines he was taking. All I knew he was taking insulin for his diabetes and that was it. I had no clue what diabetes was. To me it was just one of those popular sicknesses you hear people talk about without really knowing the cause and effect.

Mr. E repeatedly told me that he inherited his diabetes from his mother. Medical professionals and researchers say that the diabetes disease is prevalent amongst African-Caribbean and Asians people. Because we eat a lot of carbohydrates and starchy foods, such as yams, plantains and corns products. But the disease is now prevalent throughout the world especially amongst the overweight population or amongst those suffering with obesity. The problem is costing the NHS and governments around the world billions of dollars to treat the disease. I blame it on too much genitally modify foods crop.

SOLO STAR LINTUS

Mr. E's medication included Solo Star Lintus Pen Insulin. His blood sugar level needed to be monitored and tested regularly whilst using this medicine or any other forms of insulin. I got use to seeing Mr. E injecting himself or being injected with insulin by nursing professionals. While at home when his vision was impaired and he could not see properly to read his glucose level on the monitor. I had to call out the blood glucose reading to him after pricking his finger to test his blood glucose level. Once the reading was at the required level I would then dial the doses on the insulin pen and place the insulin pen in his hand in the correct manner for him to inject himself. Most times he would inject himself in the abdomen. His injection site was mainly rotated by nurses whilst in hospital. Controlling and testing blood glucose level is an ongoing feature for those with diabetes.

Solo Star Lintus Insulin is long acting insulin. According to research it is the only 24 hour approved acting insulin. It is exclusively for use of once a day. It is used as part of the diabetic treatment plan which includes diet and exercise, and with other diabetes medications and regular blood testing. Taking Solo Star Lintus just once a day helps control blood glucose all day long.

It should not be taken if you are allergic to insulin or any of the inactive ingredients in it. Your blood glucose level needs to be tested regular whilst on this insulin. You should not make any changes to your dose with this or any other types of insulin without discussing it first with your doctor or medical professionals. You should not dilute it with any other insulin or solution as it will not work as intended. And it could result in loosing blood glucose control which could be serious. Solo Star Lintus solution must be colorless with no particular visible in it. If not! Return it to your doctor or diabetic medical professional. You must not share needles, insulin pen or syringe with others.

COMMON SIDE EFFECT

The most common side effect with insulin including Solo Star Lintus is (hypoglycemia) which may be serious. Some people may experience symptoms such as shaking, sweating, fast heart beat and blurred vision. Sever hypoglycemia can be life threatening. It may cause harm to your heart and brains. Other possible side effects may include injection site reactions, changes in fat tissue, itching and rashes.

LAXIDO

Mr. E was placed on this medicine because there was a point in his diabetes treatment when he was unable to go to the toilet to relieve his bowels for over a week. This medicine is used to treat constipation that is present for a long time as well as faecal impaction. The main ingredient in this medicine is 'macrogol' it works by absorbing water into the stool and increasing the volume and water concentration of the stool. This helps relieve constipation and the stool passes through the bowel more easily. This medication is available in powder sachet that should be dissolved in water before taking it by mouth.

ALTERNATIVE MEDICATION AND HERBS

Many medical professionals say that there is no cures for diabetes. But some herbalist, or alternative medicine providers and practitioners would disagree and say that there are many preventative drugs that can eliminate, cure or reduce diabetes. One such herb is Chicory.

THE BENEFIT OF CHICORY

To my knowledge or during the time I spent with Mr. E I never witnessed him using any alternative medicine. The only drug I saw him smoking was marijuana and that was more at times of socialising and enjoyment than for any medical purpose. But like I have said before I barely knew any thing about his medical intake. I only presumed the marijuana he smoked was purely used for his pleasure. Many drugs specialist say marijuana - cannabis is good for healing people with multiplsoureses (MS) but that's another topic which I do not wish to going into.

Chicory

The medicinal usages of Chicory are enormous. Chicory works as an excellent coffee substance and contain insulin, the substance that diabetics need to remove excess glucose (sugar) from their blood. Chicory is an edible perennial herb, which means they last for more than two growing seasons, either dying after each season and growing again as most herbaceous plant do, or growing continuously as some bush do.

Chicory is a native plant of North Africa. Today it can be found all over the world. It gained its name in antiquity because of its therapeutic nature. Used by the ancient Hebrews and Egyptians to treat liver and gall-bladder problems. Chicory was consumed in large quantity by the ancient fathers, herbalist and the wider population. They believed that this herb could purify the blood and eliminate toxins in the liver.

The root of the chicory plant is used as a coffee substitute, the other parts are used in cooking, especially salads. Compared with real coffee, chicory stimulates the nervous system by its mental capabilities to aid concentration. It contains chicorine and choline. An ammonia compound soluble found in animal and plants tissue that is involved in fat transportation and its chemical formula is $C_5H_{15}N_2$.

Chicory shows laxative digestion and its pancreatic secretion regulates the glucose in the human body. If it is included in your diet the body will adjust the level of cholesterols. Cholesterols is a solid compound of fat in the blood; a steroid alcohol. The sterol made by the liver that is present in cells. Cholesterol is important to the body as a constituent of cell membranes, and is involved in the formation of bile acid and some hormones. Formula $C_{27} H_{45} OH$. Chemical compound found in insulin.

Insulin is the hormone that regulates glucose (sugar) level in the blood. It is produced by the pancreas in your body. The pancreas is a large elongated glandular organ located near your stomach. It secretes and emits juices into the small intestine such as the hormone insulin, glucagons, and somatostatin which passes into the blood stream.

CHEMICAL OF CHICORY
Somatostain is a hormone that is produced in hypothalamus that inhabits the release of growth hormone. The chemical compositions found in chicory are insulin, chicorine, choline, tannin, acid, and vitamins B, C, K, and P. Are good insulin products for diabetes?

The root of this herb contains the highest concentration of the above substances. Various studies have shown that the insulin in this plant greatly reduces the risk of intestinal cancer. Tannin is found in this herb and works as a astringent disinfectant, detoxicant tonic; and has a light antibiotic effect. It further influences the gallbladder effects by enlarging the gall and the fluid quantity. I can only suggest if you are diabetic and wish to try alternative medicines you should first consult your doctor, pharmacist or medical professional.

Many people today buy and take over the counter alternative herbal medicines because of the fear of too much artificial chemical in prescribed drug and feel that many prescribed drugs are a means of lining the pockets of big pharmaceutical companies. The argument states that most people don't know the medicinal compounds that go into making- up the medications they are prescribed. And drugs are bought and sold over the counter or on the internet like sweets. Big drug company spend hundreds of dollars advertising drugs aimed at the vulnerable such as the poor and the elderly to profit from their misfortunes. One man's misfortune often is another man's gain.

CONCLUSION

Type 2 diabetes is treated by controlling blood glucose. If glucose are not controlled with insulin, diet and exercise this can result in foot ulcer. Mr. E whom I cared for with type 2 diabetes for two years eventually develop foot ulcer and finally had to be amputated below the knees on his right foot and the removal of the two last toes on his left feet.

It has been reported by Helen Gilpin and Kate Lagan that 15% of all individuals with diabetes will experience a foot ulcer at some point in their life time. Foot ulcer can affect your quality of life if you have diabetes. They say 3.5% of people in the UK population who has diabetes has suffered from a current or previous foot ulcer. Before I was removed from caring for Mr. A, he had gone from being a perceivably normal healthy looking walking man to being amputated. I was the only person present with Mr. E in hospital when he went into surgery and when he came out of surgery for the amputation.

It was a terrible experience for himself and for me as his carer. Especially when his family removed me from caring for him about a month after his operation because I did not get to see Mr. E's completion of his treatment. Such as whether he had his prosthetic leg fitted, or whether he was sticking to his insulin treatment or if he had reduced taking some of his medicines. I returned a call to Mr. E in December 2013 to see how he was doing. He'd previously told me he wanted me to investigate his missing items from his previous landlord. In conversation Mr. E informed me that he wasn't wearing any cloths at his current place of resident neither to attend his hospital appointments except for a pair of panamas bottoms. I naturally assumed he was wearing the blue panama's bottoms I had bought for him whilst he was in hospital. I then sent out various letters on his behalf to many supporting agencies even to the Queen at Buckingham Palace to check on his health and his wellbeing.

The Discovery of insulin

Insulin was discovered by the Canadian Frederick Banting and medical student Charles H Best. Best discovered the hormone insulin in the pancreas. He first extracts from dogs with diabetes. On July 30, 1921, they injected the hormone into a diabetic dog and found it effectively lowered the dog's blood glucose level to normal. By the end of the year, with the help of Canadian chemist James B Collip and Scottish physiologist J.J Macleod. Banting and Best purified insulin and it was used to successfully treat a boy suffering from severe diabetes. The researchers were celebrated and honoured for their breakthrough. Banting and MacLeod shared the 1923 Noble Prize for Physiology and Medicine for their work.

According to the publication in Britannica pharmaceutical industry article, insulin was discovered in 1921. But in 1869 Paul Langerhans a medical student in Germany, was studying the histology of pancreas. He noted that the organ has two distinct type of cells - acinar, cell now known to secrete digestive enzymes, and islet cells (we now call it islets of Langerhans).

The function of islet cells was suggested in 1889 when German physiologist and pathologist Oskar Murkowski and German physician Joseph von Miring showed that removing the pancreas from a dog caused the animal to exhibit a disorder quite similar to human diabetes mellitus (elevated blood glucose and metabolic changes). After this discovery, a number of scientist in various part of the world attempted to extract the active substance from the pancreas so that it could be used to treat diabetes. Today call human insulin. One of those scientists was Romanian physiologist Nicolas C Paulescu. Paulescu received his education in Paris. Where he trained under French physician Etienne Lancereaux. Lancereaux had long suspected that the pancreas was the source of diabetes.

At the beginning of the 20th century, having received a doctorates in biological chemistry and the natural science from the University of Paris, Paulescu began searching for the active pancreas substance that he believe would cure diabetes. He returned to Bucharest, where working in experimental physiology at the university there, he later hypothesized that the active substance of the pancreas acts on glucose, allowing glucose to be stored in muscles and liver and when absent, resulted in the accumulation of glucose in the blood.

The discovery of insulin has come a long way. As for myself further ongoing studies into the subject of diabetes would be necessary for me to truly comprehend to nature and cures of the disease.